Editor
Mary S. Jones, M.A.

Cover Artist
Brenda DiAntonis

Managing Editor
Ina Massler Levin, M.A.

Creative Director
Karen J. Goldfluss, M.S. Ed.

Art Production Manager
Kevin Barnes

Art Coordinator
Renée Christine Yates

Imaging
Rosa C. See

Publisher

Mary D. Smith, M.S. Ed.

Daily Independent

RECORD and JOURNAL

Grades 4-7

Author

Pamela Batterbee Pierson

Teacher Created Resources, Inc.
6421 Industry Way
Westminster, CA 92683
www.teachercreated.com

ISBN: 978-1-4206-8722-4

© 2007 Teacher Created Resources, Inc.

Made in U.S.A.

Teacher Created Resources

Table of Contents

Introduction

These *Daily Independent Reading Record and Journal* pages were created to give students a more structured idea of what it means to "respond" to and be accountable for their reading. As every teacher knows, there are typically two types of students in a classroom when it comes to written responses: 1) students who can write on and on and have difficulty getting to the point, and 2) students who have great ideas and responses buried deep beneath their gentle exteriors, but "freeze" at the suggestion that they put any of those thoughts into the written word. Once in a while, we are fortunate to have students who can put their thoughts into words and transfer those words fluently onto paper. Most students, however, need our help in stimulating their thought processes and organizing those ideas into a reasonable, easy-to-understand written response.

You will find responses for three types of readings: Fiction, Nonfiction, and Content Area. Each journal page that you choose to use as a reading response in your classroom should be introduced individually with a mini-lesson. Your expectations should be thoroughly explained at the outset of every lesson, and the rubric should be presented in detail. For ease of use, the rubric should be enlarged into a poster and posted in your room for daily reference. You will find the rubric on page 5.

After you have introduced all of the daily reading responses you desire to use, the sheets may be copied and kept in a specific, accessible place so that the students may choose the response they would like to make after their daily independent reading time. Those teachers whose schools are limited in their paper supply can copy the journal pages onto different colors of paper and tell the students to "get out the ____ color for today's reading response." Do whatever works for you. The options are endless.

Please note that there are two miscellaneous forms. The "free response" form allows for individual expression/response for those students who have something to say about their book that does not fit into any of the journal pages provided. There is also an "open form" for the teacher to complete to his/her specifications and distribute. In the Resources section at the back of the book, there is a master copy of lines (page 77) that may be printed on the back of the journal pages for additional writing space, along with a T-Graph (page 78), a Vocabulary Definition/Sketch Chart (page 79), and a KWL Chart (page 80). Those pages that require a chart to be copied to the back are indicated with instructions for the teacher at the bottom of the page.

Introduction *(cont.)*

Benefits of Using the Journal Pages

- The students are given prompts along with some structure to encourage and guide them in their responses to what they've read.
- These are single half-sheets that may be turned in on a daily basis and cut copying time in half.
- They are not bulky (like composition books) or cumbersome to collect.
- Parents see their child's work on a daily or weekly basis, rather than at the end of the unit or year as with lengthy notebooks. This is especially important if you plan to calculate grades or create progress reports.
- There is an easy-to-follow rubric that makes grading the pages less subjective and easy to assess.

Suggestions for Teaching the Journal Pages

Before assigning any journal pages, it is suggested that you model three very specific skills required: rephrasing, referring to the passage, and elaboration.

✏ Rephrasing

One of the quickest and easiest ways to teach a child to write their answers in comprehensive, complete sentences is to teach them to rephrase each questions or instructional statement into part of the answer. Some of the instructions ask for the students to make an illustration, graphic organizer, or put a check next to a choice. However, most of the instructional statements ask the students to respond in writing. In responding, they should rephrase their instructions as part of their answer.

For example: If the instructions say to "Close your book and make a prediction about what will happen next," the students' responses should begin something like this:

  a. My prediction about what will happen next is . . .

  b. I predict that the next thing that will happen is . . .

✏ Referring to the Passage

Another common requirement in state and national testing is that writers "prove" the accuracy of their responses by referring to the facts in the article on which they are working. By requiring students to cite information in their daily responses, you are teaching them that referring to the passage for answering questions is often essential to proving your point and/or insuring accuracy. If students learn to do so on a daily basis, it should become an "automatic" focus when testing occurs—whether it's in the classroom or during state/national testing.

✏ Elaboration

Elaboration can be used in two basic forms:

  1. Giving more details. For example: In giving the setting, a student might simply state that the story takes place in Arkansas. A student who elaborates would tell you that the story takes place in the spring of 1819 on a small family farm in the back hills of Siloam Springs, Arkansas.

  2. Interjecting personal thoughts. For example: As he/she is referring to the passage, a student might explain what he/she thinks is meant by a certain comment, express empathy for a character who is experiencing trauma, or share a similar experience. He/she relates a situation that is similar to one a character is experiencing in the story.

Each journal page should be completed with rephrasing as often as possible, and at least one or both of the other two skills (referring to the passage or elaboration), as applicable. You will notice that referring to the passage and elaboration are significant aspects of the rubric scoring. Therefore, it would be advisable to make reviewing these skills a part of every lesson for the first four to six weeks.

Features of the Journal Pages

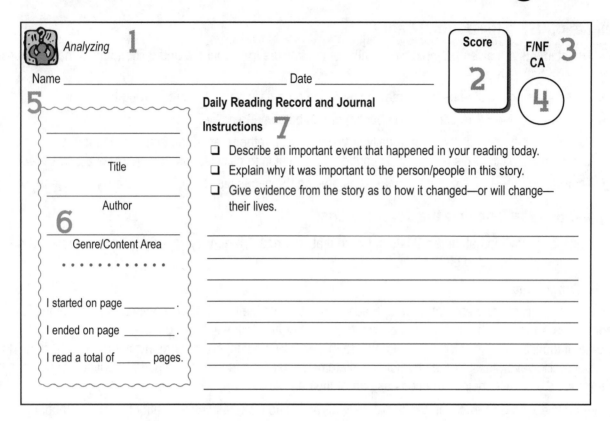

1. Quick Category Reference: For teachers and students to know the topic of the questions.

2. Score Box: For teachers to write the student's score for each journal page.

3. Quick Genre Reference: For teachers to know what kind of reading material works with each journal page. F = Fiction, NF = Nonfiction, CA = Content Area

4. Page Number: For students to keep their journal pages in order.

5. Record-Keeping Box: For students to complete specific information about the book they read each day.

6. Genre/Content Area: For students to indicate a more specific genre (e.g., realistic fiction, historical fiction, bibliography, etc.) or content area (e.g., science, social studies, etc.).

7. Step-by-Step Instructions: Includes blank boxes next to each one for checking off as each instruction is followed.

Scoring Rubric

Grade Equivalent	Score	Requirements
95%	4	• All directions for that day are addressed in the answer. • Thoughts are expressed clearly and indicate excellent comprehension about what was read. • Includes appropriate references to the passage. • Excellent elaboration—may be beyond the literal. • Turned in on time.
85%	3	• All or most directions for the day are addressed in the answer. • Thoughts are expressed well and indicate clear comprehension about what was read. • Includes adequate references to the passage. • Good attempt(s) made to elaborate. • Scored a 4, but turned in late.
75%	2	• Some or most of the directions for that day are addressed in the answer. • Thoughts are not expressed well and/or indicate unclear comprehension or confusion about what was read. • Only one, or poor references. • Little or no attempt at elaboration. • Scored a 3, but turned in late.
65%	1	• Directions are inadequately followed. • Thoughts are expressed poorly and/or indicate a significant measure of confusion about what was read. • No references. • No elaboration. • Scored a 2, but turned in late.
0	0	• No attempt. • Did not turn in paper.

Plus, one point each for:

_____ Information completed   _____ Spelling/Grammar   _____ Capitalization/Punctuation
(name, date, book info., etc.)

_____ Neatness   _____ Sentence Structure

Example: If a student receives a score of **3** for the journal page requirements, it would be a grade equivalent of **85%**. Additional points may be added to his/her grade equivalent for each of the five skills listed above. For instance, if the student displayed good sentence structure, capitalization/punctuation, and neatness—but did not compete all of the information and was careless in spelling (1) words that a student his/her age should know how to spell and (2) names or words taken straight from the book—the student would receive an additional **3** out of a possible 5 additional points, to equal **88%**.

Interest Survey

Name _____ Date _____

Daily Reading Record and Journal

Instructions

❑ Write a letter to your teacher expressing how you feel about reading.

❑ You may be totally honest. Explain what you like and dislike about reading.

_____

_____

_____

_____

_____

_____

_____

_____

_____

- -

Interest Survey

Name _____ Date _____

Score

Daily Reading Record and Journal

Instructions

❑ Write a letter to your teacher expressing how you feel about reading.

❑ You may be totally honest. Explain what you like and dislike about reading.

_____

_____

_____

_____

_____

_____

_____

_____

Interest Survey

Score

Name _____ Date _____

Daily Reading Record and Journal

Instructions

❑ Write a letter to your teacher expressing whether you consider yourself a strong reader, an average reader, or a struggling reader.

❑ Explain what you do well as a reader.

❑ List two things you need to work on to become a better reader.

_____
_____
_____
_____
_____
_____
_____
_____
_____

- -

Interest Survey

Score

Name _____ Date _____

Daily Reading Record and Journal

Instructions

❑ Write a letter to your teacher expressing whether you consider yourself a strong reader, an average reader, or a struggling reader.

❑ Explain what you do well as a reader.

❑ List two things you need to work on to become a better reader.

_____
_____
_____
_____
_____
_____
_____

Interest Survey

Name _____ Date _____

Daily Reading Record and Journal

Instructions

- ❏ Write a letter to your teacher identifying your favorite genre (fantasy, realistic fiction, biography, etc.).
- ❏ Explain why you prefer the genre and what you like most about it.
- ❏ Give three examples of books or scenes you especially enjoyed from that genre.

_____

_____

_____

_____

_____

_____

_____

_____

- -

Interest Survey

Score

Name _____ Date _____

Daily Reading Record and Journal

Instructions

- ❏ Write a letter to your teacher identifying your favorite genre (fantasy, realistic fiction, biography, etc.).
- ❏ Explain why you prefer the genre and what you like most about it.
- ❏ Give three examples of books or scenes you especially enjoyed from that genre.

_____

_____

_____

_____

_____

_____

_____

_____

Interest Survey

Name _____ Date _____

_____
_____
Title

_____
Author

_____
Genre

Daily Reading Record and Journal

Instructions

❑ Write the name of your favorite book in the box. If you remember the author's name, write that in also. Indicate its genre.

❑ Explain why it is your favorite.

❑ Summarize the story in 5–8 sentences.

_____
_____

_____
_____
_____
_____
_____
_____
_____

- -

Interest Survey

Score

Name _____ Date _____

_____
_____
Title

_____
Author

_____
Genre

Daily Reading Record and Journal

Instructions

❑ Write the name of your favorite book in the box. If you remember the author's name, write that in also. Indicate its genre.

❑ Explain why it is your favorite.

❑ Summarize the story in 5–8 sentences.

_____
_____

_____
_____
_____
_____
_____
_____

Pre-Reading

Name _____ Date _____

NF/CA

_____

_____
Title

_____
Author

_____
Genre/Content Area

• • • • • • • • • • •

I started on page _____ .

I ended on page _____ .

I read a total of _____ pages.

Daily Reading Record and Journal

Instructions

❑ Briefly describe the cover of your book.

❑ Survey your book by reading the: _____ title

_____ back cover

_____ first page of the first chapter

❑ List at least three things you think you will learn by reading this book.

_____

_____

_____

_____

_____

_____

_____

- -

Pre-Reading

Name _____ Date _____

Score NF/CA

_____

_____
Title

_____
Author

_____
Genre/Content Area

• • • • • • • • • • •

I started on page _____ .

I ended on page _____ .

I read a total of _____ pages.

Daily Reading Record and Journal

Instructions

❑ Briefly describe the cover of your book.

❑ Survey your book by reading the: _____ title

_____ back cover

_____ first page of the first chapter

❑ List at least three things you think you will learn by reading this book.

_____

_____

_____

_____

_____

_____

_____

Pre-Reading

Score CA

Name _____ Date _____

Daily Reading Record and Journal

_____
_____
Title

_____
Author

_____
Content Area

• • • • • • • • • • •

I started on page _____ .

I ended on page _____ .

I read a total of _____ pages.

Instructions

❑ Survey the chapter by: _____ reading the title

_____ looking at the pictures and reading their captions

_____ reading subtitles, vocabulary words, and any other bold or italicized print

❑ Write at least three questions you think will be answered as you read the chapter.

_____
_____
_____
_____
_____
_____
_____

- -

Pre-Reading

Score CA

Name _____ Date _____

Daily Reading Record and Journal

_____
_____
Title

_____
Author

_____
Content Area

• • • • • • • • • • •

I started on page _____ .

I ended on page _____ .

I read a total of _____ pages.

Instructions

❑ Survey the chapter by: _____ reading the title

_____ looking at the pictures and reading their captions

_____ reading subtitles, vocabulary words, and any other bold or italicized print

❑ Write at least three questions you think will be answered as you read the chapter.

_____
_____
_____
_____
_____
_____

Pre-Reading

Name _____ Date _____

_____

_____

Title

_____

Author

_____

Genre/Content Area

• • • • • • • • • • •

I started on page _____ .

I ended on page _____ .

I read a total of _____ pages.

Daily Reading Record and Journal

Instructions

We choose books for many different reasons such as recommendations, attractive cover, genre, intriguing paragraphs on the back or inside cover, great illustrations, etc.

❑ Explain why you chose to read this book.

❑ Identify what parts of the book you looked at or read before deciding to read it.

_____

_____

_____

_____

_____

_____

_____

- -

Pre-Reading

Name _____ Date _____

_____

_____

Title

_____

Author

_____

Genre/Content Area

• • • • • • • • • • •

I started on page _____ .

I ended on page _____ .

I read a total of _____ pages.

Daily Reading Record and Journal

Instructions

We choose books for many different reasons such as recommendations, attractive cover, genre, intriguing paragraphs on the back or inside cover, great illustrations, etc.

❑ Explain why you chose to read this book.

❑ Identify what parts of the book you looked at or read before deciding to read it.

_____

_____

_____

_____

_____

_____

_____

Pre-Reading

Name _____ Date _____

_____

_____

Title

_____

Author

_____

Content Area

• • • • • • • • • • • •

I started on page _____ .

I ended on page _____ .

I read a total of _____ pages.

Daily Reading Record and Journal

Instructions

❑ Topic/Subject:_____

❑ **Before reading:** Create a KWL chart on the back and fill in what you already <u>know</u> (K) about this topic/subject and two things that you <u>want</u> (W) to know about it.

❑ **After reading:** Fill in the "L" column detailing what you <u>learned</u>.

❑ On the lines below, write a brief paragraph explaining whether or not any of the items in your "W" column were answered in your reading.

_____

_____

_____

_____

_____

(Copy KWL chart, page 80, on the back).

Pre-Reading

Name _____ Date _____

_____

_____

Title

_____

Author

_____

Content Area

• • • • • • • • • • • •

I started on page _____ .

I ended on page _____ .

I read a total of _____ pages.

Daily Reading Record and Journal

Instructions

❑ Topic/Subject:_____

❑ **Before reading:** Create a KWL chart on the back and fill in what you already <u>know</u> (K) about this topic/subject and two things that you <u>want</u> (W) to know about it.

❑ **After reading:** Fill in the "L" column detailing what you <u>learned</u>.

❑ On the lines below, write a brief paragraph explaining whether or not any of the items in your "W" column were answered in your reading.

_____

_____

_____

_____

_____

(Copy KWL chart, page 80, on the back).

Analyzing

Name _____ Date _____

_____
Title

_____
Author

_____
Genre/Content Area

• • • • • • • • • • • •

I started on page _____ .

I ended on page _____ .

I read a total of _____ pages.

Daily Reading Record and Journal

Instructions

❏ Describe an important event that happened in your reading today.

❏ Explain why it was important to the character(s) in this story.

❏ Give evidence from the story as to how it changed—or will change— their lives.

_____

_____

_____

_____

_____

_____

_____

_____

- -

Analyzing

Name _____ Date _____

_____
Title

_____
Author

_____
Genre/Content Area

• • • • • • • • • • • •

I started on page _____ .

I ended on page _____ .

I read a total of _____ pages.

Daily Reading Record and Journal

Instructions

❏ Describe an important event that happened in your reading today.

❏ Explain why it was important to the character(s) in this story.

❏ Give evidence from the story as to how it changed—or will change— their lives.

_____

_____

_____

_____

_____

_____

_____

_____

Analyzing

Name _____ Date _____

Daily Reading Record and Journal

_____

Title

_____

Author

_____

Genre

. . . .

I started on page _____ .

I ended on page _____ .

I read a total of _____ pages.

Instructions

❑ Outline the main events that have taken place in this story so far.

❑ Explain why you think those events could or could not happen today.

_____

_____

_____

_____

_____

_____

_____

_____

_____

- -

Analyzing

Name _____ Date _____

Daily Reading Record and Journal

_____

Title

_____

Author

_____

Genre

. . . .

I started on page _____ .

I ended on page _____ .

I read a total of _____ pages.

Instructions

❑ Outline the main events that have taken place in this story so far.

❑ Explain why you think those events could or could not happen today.

_____

_____

_____

_____

_____

_____

_____

_____

_____

Analyzing

Name _____ Date _____

Daily Reading Record and Journal

_____
Title

_____
Author

_____
Genre

• • • • • • • • • • • •

I started on page _____ .

I ended on page _____ .

I read a total of _____ pages.

Instructions

❑ Explain about a life lesson people should learn from this story.

❑ Support your answer with several pieces of evidence from the book.

❑ Explain why it is an important lesson to you and how it will help you.

_____

_____

_____

_____

_____

_____

_____

_____

Analyzing

Name _____ Date _____

Daily Reading Record and Journal

_____
Title

_____
Author

_____
Genre

• • • • • • • • • • • •

I started on page _____ .

I ended on page _____ .

I read a total of _____ pages.

Instructions

❑ Explain about a life lesson people should learn from this story.

❑ Support your answer with several pieces of evidence from the book.

❑ Explain why it is an important lesson to you and how it will help you.

_____

_____

_____

_____

_____

_____

_____

_____

Analyzing

Name _____ Date _____

F/NF
CA

Daily Reading Record and Journal

_____
Title

_____
Author

_____
Genre/Content Area

. . . .

I started on page _____ .

I ended on page _____ .

I read a total of _____ pages.

Instructions

❑ As you're reading today, mark any causes you find with a sticky note. Look for signal words, such as *because*, *so*, *as a result*, *therefore*, *if/then*, etc.

❑ Think about how each cause changed things and create a T-graph that outlines the causes and their effects in this passage.

Cause	Effect
•	•

(Copy T-graph, page 78, on the back.)

Analyzing

Name _____ Date _____

Score

F/NF
CA

Daily Reading Record and Journal

_____
Title

_____
Author

_____
Genre/Content Area

. . . .

I started on page _____ .

I ended on page _____ .

I read a total of _____ pages.

Instructions

❑ As you're reading today, mark any causes you find with a sticky note. Look for signal words, such as *because*, *so*, *as a result*, *therefore*, *if/then*, etc.

❑ Think about how each cause changed things and create a T-graph that outlines the causes and their effects in this passage.

Cause	Effect
•	•

(Copy T-graph, page 78, on the back.)

Analyzing

Score   F/NF

Name _____ Date _____

Daily Reading Record and Journal

_____

_____

Title

_____

Author

_____

Genre

• • • • • • • • • • •

I started on page _____ .

I ended on page _____ .

I read a total of _____ pages.

Instructions

❏ Write a paragraph explaining how the book and the movie are alike.

❏ Write a second paragraph explaining how the book and the movie are different.

❏ Write a third paragraph explaining which one you like the best and why.

_____

_____

_____

_____

_____

_____

_____

_____

_____

- -

Analyzing

Score   F/NF

Name _____ Date _____

Daily Reading Record and Journal

_____

_____

Title

_____

Author

_____

Genre

• • • • • • • • • • •

I started on page _____ .

I ended on page _____ .

I read a total of _____ pages.

Instructions

❏ Write a paragraph explaining how the book and the movie are alike.

❏ Write a second paragraph explaining how the book and the movie are different.

❏ Write a third paragraph explaining which one you like the best and why.

_____

_____

_____

_____

_____

_____

_____

_____

Score   **F/NF**

Name _____ Date _____

Daily Reading Record and Journal

_____
Title

_____
Author

_____
Genre

• • • • • • • • • • •

I started on page _____ .

I ended on page _____ .

I read a total of _____ pages.

Instructions

❑ If you could make this book into a movie, what scene would you use to open the movie? Would you start the movie on page one?

❑ Describe the scene in detail.

❑ Explain why you think this scene would grab the audience's attention and interest.

_____

_____

_____

_____

_____

_____

_____

- -

Analyzing

Score   **F/NF**

Name _____ Date _____

Daily Reading Record and Journal

_____
Title

_____
Author

_____
Genre

• • • • • • • • • • •

I started on page _____ .

I ended on page _____ .

I read a total of _____ pages.

Instructions

❑ If you could make this book into a movie, what scene would you use to open the movie? Would you start the movie on page one?

❑ Describe the scene in detail.

❑ Explain why you think this scene would grab the audience's attention and interest.

_____

_____

_____

_____

_____

_____

_____

Analyzing

Name _____ Date _____

Score   F/NF

Daily Reading Record and Journal

Instructions

❑ Explain how reading this book helped you. Think about the lessons you learned from the characters/people or life situations in this book.

❑ Express how you felt and what you thought when you read about their choices and experiences.

❑ Be sure to support your thoughts with examples from the passage.

_____

_____

_____

_____

_____

_____

_____

_____

_____

_____

Title

_____

Author

_____

Genre

• • • • • • • • • • • •

I started on page _____ .

I ended on page _____ .

I read a total of _____ pages.

Analyzing

Name _____ Date _____

Score   F/NF

Daily Reading Record and Journal

Instructions

❑ Explain how reading this book helped you. Think about the lessons you learned from the characters/people or life situations in this book.

❑ Express how you felt and what you thought when you read about their choices and experiences.

❑ Be sure to support your thoughts with examples from the passage.

_____

_____

_____

_____

_____

_____

_____

_____

_____

Title

_____

Author

_____

Genre

• • • • • • • • • • • •

I started on page _____ .

I ended on page _____ .

I read a total of _____ pages.

Analyzing

Name _____ Date _____

Daily Reading Record and Journal

_____
Title

_____
Author

_____
Genre

• • • • • • • • • • • •

I started on page _____ .

I ended on page _____ .

I read a total of _____ pages.

Instructions

❑ Copy 3–5 sentences from your book that contain figurative language, such as metaphors, similes, idioms, etc.

❑ Underline the portion of each sentence that is figurative.

❑ Explain what you think each phrase means. Look for context clues to help you.

_____

_____

_____

_____

_____

_____

Analyzing

Name _____ Date _____

Daily Reading Record and Journal

_____
Title

_____
Author

_____
Genre

• • • • • • • • • • • •

I started on page _____ .

I ended on page _____ .

I read a total of _____ pages.

Instructions

❑ Copy 3–5 sentences from your book that contain figurative language, such as metaphors, similes, idioms, etc.

❑ Underline the portion of each sentence that is figurative.

❑ Explain what you think each phrase means. Look for context clues to help you.

_____

_____

_____

_____

_____

_____

Analyzing

Name _____ Date _____

_____

_____
Title

_____
Author

_____
Genre/Content Area

• • • • • • • • • • • • •

I started on page _____ .

I ended on page _____ .

I read a total of _____ pages.

Daily Reading Record and Journal

Instructions

❑   Topic/Subject of today's reading: _____

❑   Describe how the information in this book could help you outside of school.

_____

_____

_____

_____

_____

_____

_____

_____

_____

- -

Analyzing

Name _____ Date _____

_____

_____
Title

_____
Author

_____
Genre/Content Area

• • • • • • • • • • • • •

I started on page _____ .

I ended on page _____ .

I read a total of _____ pages.

Daily Reading Record and Journal

Instructions

❑   Topic/Subject of today's reading: _____

❑   Describe how the information in this book could help you outside of school.

_____

_____

_____

_____

_____

_____

_____

_____

_____

Analyzing

Name _____ Date _____

Daily Reading Record and Journal

_____
Title

_____
Author

_____
Genre/Content Area

• • • • • • • • • • • •

I started on page _____ .

I ended on page _____ .

I read a total of _____ pages.

Instructions

❑ Topic/Subject of today's reading: _____

❑ Describe any graphics or other tools the author could have used to make the information easier to understand.

❑ Include an example of what you mean on the back.

_____

_____

_____

_____

_____

_____

_____

(Do not copy lines on the back of this page.)

- -

Analyzing

Name _____ Date _____

Score   NF/CA

Daily Reading Record and Journal

_____
Title

_____
Author

_____
Genre/Content Area

• • • • • • • • • • • •

I started on page _____ .

I ended on page _____ .

I read a total of _____ pages.

Instructions

❑ Topic/Subject of today's reading: _____

❑ Describe any graphics or other tools the author could have used to make the information easier to understand.

❑ Include an example of what you mean on the back.

_____

_____

_____

_____

_____

_____

_____

(Do not copy lines on the back of this page.)

Analyzing

Name _____ Date _____

_____

_____
Title

_____
Author

_____
Content Area

. . . .

I started on page _____ .

I ended on page _____ .

I read a total of _____ pages.

Daily Reading Record and Journal

Instructions

❑ Topic/Subject:_____

❑ Find two aspects of today's reading that would be interesting to compare and contrast. For example: mammals and reptiles. Create a graphic organizer on the back of this page to assemble the information.

❑ Write a brief paragraph on the front of this page to explain your findings.

_____

_____

_____

_____

_____

_____

(Do not copy lines on the back of this page.)

- -

Analyzing

Name _____ Date _____

_____

_____
Title

_____
Author

_____
Content Area

. . . .

I started on page _____ .

I ended on page _____ .

I read a total of _____ pages.

Daily Reading Record and Journal

Instructions

❑ Topic/Subject:_____

❑ Find two aspects of today's reading that would be interesting to compare and contrast. For example: mammals and reptiles. Create a graphic organizer on the back of this page to assemble the information.

❑ Write a brief paragraph on the front of this page to explain your findings.

_____

_____

_____

_____

_____

_____

(Do not copy lines on the back of this page.)

Author's Craft

Name _____ Date _____

Score **F/NF**

Daily Reading Record and Journal

_____

_____
Title

_____
Author

_____
Genre

• • • • • • • • • • •

I started on page _____ .

I ended on page _____ .

I read a total of _____ pages.

Instructions

❑ Explain why you think the author did or did not do a good job writing this story.

❑ Give examples from the book to prove your point of view.

❑ Tell if you would or would not like to read any other books by this author and why.

_____

_____

_____

_____

_____

_____

_____

- -

Author's Craft

Name _____ Date _____

Score **F/NF**

Daily Reading Record and Journal

_____

_____
Title

_____
Author

_____
Genre

• • • • • • • • • • •

I started on page _____ .

I ended on page _____ .

I read a total of _____ pages.

Instructions

❑ Explain why you think the author did or did not do a good job writing this story.

❑ Give examples from the book to prove your point of view.

❑ Tell if you would or would not like to read any other books by this author and why.

_____

_____

_____

_____

_____

_____

_____

Author's Craft

Score   F/NF

Name _____ Date _____

Daily Reading Record and Journal

_____
Title

_____
Author

_____
Genre

· · · · · · · · · · · ·

I started on page _____ .

I ended on page _____ .

I read a total of _____ pages.

Instructions

❑ Identify a person, idea, or event that the author wrote into the story that surprised you.

❑ Explain why you were surprised by it and what you would have expected instead.

_____
_____
_____
_____
_____
_____
_____
_____
_____

- -

Author's Craft

Score   F/NF

Name _____ Date _____

Daily Reading Record and Journal

_____
Title

_____
Author

_____
Genre

· · · · · · · · · · · ·

I started on page _____ .

I ended on page _____ .

I read a total of _____ pages.

Instructions

❑ Identify a person, idea, or event that the author wrote into the story that surprised you.

❑ Explain why you were surprised by it and what you would have expected instead.

_____
_____
_____
_____
_____
_____
_____
_____
_____

Author's Craft

Name _____ Date _____

Score | **F/NF CA**

Title
_____

Author
_____

Genre/Content Area

• • • • • • • • • • • •

I started on page _____ .

I ended on page _____ .

I read a total of _____ pages.

Daily Reading Record and Journal

Instructions

❑ Identify the author's purpose for writing this piece:

____ to teach a lesson   ____ to persuade/dissuade   ____ to entertain

❑ Give details from the writing that proves the author succeeded.

_____

_____

_____

_____

_____

_____

_____

_____

Author's Craft

Name _____ Date _____

Score | **F/NF CA**

Title
_____

Author
_____

Genre/Content Area

• • • • • • • • • • • •

I started on page _____ .

I ended on page _____ .

I read a total of _____ pages.

Daily Reading Record and Journal

Instructions

❑ Identify the author's purpose for writing this piece:

____ to teach a lesson   ____ to persuade/dissuade   ____ to entertain

❑ Give details from the writing that proves the author succeeded.

_____

_____

_____

_____

_____

_____

_____

_____

Author's Craft

Name _____ Date _____

_____

_____

Title

_____

Author

_____

Genre

• • • • • • • • • • •

I started on page _____ .

I ended on page _____ .

I read a total of _____ pages.

Daily Reading Record and Journal

Instructions

❏ Identify one special technique the author uses in his/her writing style, such as figurative language, visual images, humor, flashing back in time, etc.

❏ Give several examples from the story.

❏ Explain whether or not you think the technique made the story better and why.

_____

_____

_____

_____

_____

_____

_____

Author's Craft

Name _____ Date _____

_____

_____

Title

_____

Author

_____

Genre

• • • • • • • • • • •

I started on page _____ .

I ended on page _____ .

I read a total of _____ pages.

Daily Reading Record and Journal

Instructions

❏ Identify one special technique the author uses in his/her writing style, such as figurative language, visual images, humor, flashing back in time, etc.

❏ Give several examples from the story.

❏ Explain whether or not you think the technique made the story better and why.

_____

_____

_____

_____

_____

_____

_____

Author's Craft

Score **F/NF**

Name _____ Date _____

Daily Reading Record and Journal

_____

_____
Title

_____
Author

_____
Genre

· · · · · · · · · · · ·

I started on page _____ .

I ended on page _____ .

I read a total of _____ pages.

Instructions

❑ Write a letter to the author telling and/or asking him/her anything that's on your mind regarding this story.

It can include a particular part you liked, something you didn't understand, questions about the author's life or writing style, his/her likes and dislikes, etc.

_____
_____
_____
_____
_____
_____
_____
_____

- -

Author's Craft

Score **F/NF**

Name _____ Date _____

Daily Reading Record and Journal

_____

_____
Title

_____
Author

_____
Genre

· · · · · · · · · · · ·

I started on page _____ .

I ended on page _____ .

I read a total of _____ pages.

Instructions

❑ Write a letter to the author telling and/or asking him/her anything that's on your mind regarding this story.

It can include a particular part you liked, something you didn't understand, questions about the author's life or writing style, his/her likes and dislikes, etc.

_____
_____
_____
_____
_____
_____
_____
_____

Author's Craft

Name _____ Date _____

_____
_____
Title

_____
Author

_____
Genre

• • • • • • • • • • • •

I started on page _____ .

I ended on page _____ .

I read a total of _____ pages.

Daily Reading Record and Journal

Instructions

❑ Think about the author's use of word choice (selective words or phrases) to create visual images, insert humor, or deepen your understanding, etc. Copy three examples.

❑ Explain how his/her word choices affected you as you read.

_____

_____

_____

_____

_____

_____

_____

_____

_____

- -

Author's Craft

Name _____ Date _____

_____
_____
Title

_____
Author

_____
Genre

• • • • • • • • • • • •

I started on page _____ .

I ended on page _____ .

I read a total of _____ pages.

Daily Reading Record and Journal

Instructions

❑ Think about the author's use of word choice (selective words or phrases) to create visual images, insert humor, or deepen your understanding, etc. Copy three examples.

❑ Explain how his/her word choices affected you as you read.

_____

_____

_____

_____

_____

_____

_____

_____

_____

Author's Craft

Name _____ Date _____

_____

_____
Title

_____
Author

_____
Genre

. . . .

I started on page _____ .

I ended on page _____ .

I read a total of _____ pages.

Daily Reading Record and Journal

Instructions

❑ Find three sentences that contain examples of word choices (selective words or phrases) the author used to help you "experience" the story. Think about words that helped you see, hear, smell, taste, or feel what was happening in the story.

❑ Copy them and underline the word choices.

_____

_____

_____

_____

_____

_____

_____

_____

- -

Author's Craft

Name _____ Date _____

_____

_____
Title

_____
Author

_____
Genre

. . . .

I started on page _____ .

I ended on page _____ .

I read a total of _____ pages.

Daily Reading Record and Journal

Instructions

❑ Find three sentences that contain examples of word choices (selective words or phrases) the author used to help you "experience" the story. Think about words that helped you see, hear, smell, taste, or feel what was happening in the story.

❑ Copy them and underline the word choices.

_____

_____

_____

_____

_____

_____

_____

_____

Character Study

Name _____ Date _____

Score   F/NF

Daily Reading Record and Journal

Instructions

- ❑ Describe one of the main characters using at least three or four details about him/her.
- ❑ Would you want to be friends with this character? ____ yes ____ no
- ❑ Explain why you would or would not want this character for a friend.

_____
_____
_____
_____
_____
_____
_____
_____
_____

_____
Title

_____
Author

_____
Genre

• • • • • • • • • •

I started on page _____ .

I ended on page _____ .

I read a total of _____ pages.

- -

Character Study

Name _____ Date _____

Score   F/NF

Daily Reading Record and Journal

Instructions

- ❑ Describe one of the main characters using at least three or four details about him/her.
- ❑ Would you want to be friends with this character? ____ yes ____ no
- ❑ Explain why you would or would not want this character for a friend.

_____
_____
_____
_____
_____
_____
_____
_____

_____
Title

_____
Author

_____
Genre

• • • • • • • • • •

I started on page _____ .

I ended on page _____ .

I read a total of _____ pages.

Character Study

Name _____ Date _____

Daily Reading Record and Journal

_____
Title

_____
Author

_____
Genre

. . . .

I started on page _____ .

I ended on page _____ .

I read a total of _____ pages.

Instructions

❑ Name one of the characters in your text:_____

❑ Describe two or more character traits that you think define the character.

❑ Support your opinion with evidence from the text.

_____

_____

_____

_____

_____

_____

_____

_____

_____

Character Study

Name _____ Date _____

Score   F/NF

Daily Reading Record and Journal

_____
Title

_____
Author

_____
Genre

. . . .

I started on page _____ .

I ended on page _____ .

I read a total of _____ pages.

Instructions

❑ Name one of the characters in your text:_____

❑ Describe two or more character traits that you think define the character.

❑ Support your opinion with evidence from the text.

_____

_____

_____

_____

_____

_____

_____

_____

_____

Character Study

Name _____ Date _____

_____

_____
Title

_____
Author

_____
Genre

• • • • • • • • • • •

I started on page _____ .

I ended on page _____ .

I read a total of _____ pages.

Daily Reading Record and Journal

Instructions

❑ Create a graphic organizer on the back to compare and contrast the main character's personality and life experiences with your personality and life experiences. Be sure to include as many details as possible.

❑ Explain it in a brief paragraph below.

_____

_____

_____

_____

_____

_____

_____

(Do not copy lines on the back of this page.)

- -

Character Study

Name _____ Date _____

_____

_____
Title

_____
Author

_____
Genre

• • • • • • • • • • •

I started on page _____ .

I ended on page _____ .

I read a total of _____ pages.

Daily Reading Record and Journal

Instructions

❑ Create a graphic organizer on the back to compare and contrast the main character's personality and life experiences with your personality and life experiences. Be sure to include as many details as possible.

❑ Explain it in a brief paragraph below.

_____

_____

_____

_____

_____

_____

_____

(Do not copy lines on the back of this page.)

Character Study

Name _____ Date _____

_____

_____
Title

_____
Author

_____
Genre

. . . .

I started on page _____ .

I ended on page _____ .

I read a total of _____ pages.

Daily Reading Record and Journal

Instructions

❑ Choose a character/person from your story: _____

❑ On the left side of the T-graph, list three character traits and/or physical attributes that you feel describe the character you chose.

❑ On the right side, defend each character trait with evidence from the book.

Trait/Attribute | Evidence
• | •

(Copy T-graph, page 78, on the back.)

Character Study

Name _____ Date _____

_____

_____
Title

_____
Author

_____
Genre

. . . .

I started on page _____ .

I ended on page _____ .

I read a total of _____ pages.

Daily Reading Record and Journal

Instructions

❑ Choose a character/person from your story: _____

❑ On the left side of the T-graph, list three character traits and/or physical attributes that you feel describe the character you chose.

❑ On the right side, defend each character trait with evidence from the book.

Trait/Attribute | Evidence
• | •

(Copy T-graph, page 78, on the back.)

Character Study

Name _____ Date _____

Daily Reading Record and Journal

_____
Title

_____
Author

_____
Genre

. . . .

I started on page _____ .

I ended on page _____ .

I read a total of _____ pages.

Instructions

❑   Identify an important (good or bad) character in this book who is not the main character and describe him/her/it.

❑   Describe his/her/its connection to the main character.

❑   Explain what makes this character's role important to the storyline of this book.

_____

_____

_____

_____

_____

_____

- -

Character Study

Name _____ Date _____

Daily Reading Record and Journal

_____
Title

_____
Author

_____
Genre

. . . .

I started on page _____ .

I ended on page _____ .

I read a total of _____ pages.

Instructions

❑   Identify an important (good or bad) character in this book who is not the main character and describe him/her/it.

❑   Describe his/her/its connection to the main character.

❑   Explain what makes this character's role important to the storyline of this book.

_____

_____

_____

_____

_____

_____

Comprehension

Name _____ Date _____

_____
_____
Title

_____
Author

_____
Content Area

· · · · · · · · · · · ·

I started on page _____ .

I ended on page _____ .

I read a total of _____ pages.

Daily Reading Record and Journal

Instructions

❑   What is the topic of your text? _____

❑   **Before reading:** Write a paragraph detailing everything you already know about the topic.

❑   **After reading:** Write a second paragraph outlining at least one fact that you learned. Add as much detail as you can remember and use only information taken from the text.

_____
_____
_____
_____
_____
_____

- -

Comprehension

Name _____ Date _____

_____
Title

_____
Author

_____
Content Area

· · · · · · · · · · · ·

I started on page _____ .

I ended on page _____ .

I read a total of _____ pages.

Daily Reading Record and Journal

Instructions

❑   What is the topic of your text? _____

❑   **Before reading:** Write a paragraph detailing everything you already know about the topic.

❑   **After reading:** Write a second paragraph outlining at least one fact that you learned. Add as much detail as you can remember and use only information taken from the text.

_____
_____
_____
_____
_____
_____

Comprehension

Name _____ Date _____

CA

Daily Reading Record and Journal

_____

Title

_____

Author

_____

Content Area

• • • • • • • • • • •

I started on page _____ .

I ended on page _____ .

I read a total of _____ pages.

Instructions

❑ Write in the topic for today's reading: _____

❑ Explain the information that was easy for you to understand.

❑ Identify the information that confused you: terms you need to have explained more clearly, facts you don't fully understand, questions you have, etc.

_____

_____

_____

_____

_____

_____

_____

Comprehension

Name _____ Date _____

Score

CA

Daily Reading Record and Journal

_____

Title

_____

Author

_____

Content Area

• • • • • • • • • • •

I started on page _____ .

I ended on page _____ .

I read a total of _____ pages.

Instructions

❑ Write in the topic for today's reading: _____

❑ Explain the information that was easy for you to understand.

❑ Identify the information that confused you: terms you need to have explained more clearly, facts you don't fully understand, questions you have, etc.

_____

_____

_____

_____

_____

_____

_____

Comprehension

Name _____ Date _____

Daily Reading Record and Journal

_____
Title

_____
Author

_____
Content Area

. . . .

I started on page _____ .

I ended on page _____ .

I read a total of _____ pages.

Instructions

❑ Topic/Subject:_____

❑ Read the passage and summarize what you read on the front side of this paper.

❑ Find a partner, trade papers, and read each other's summaries.

❑ Develop three test questions with your partner. You should each copy the questions on the back of your papers. Staple both papers together and turn them in.

_____

_____

_____

_____

_____

Comprehension

Name _____ Date _____

Daily Reading Record and Journal

_____
Title

_____
Author

_____
Content Area

. . . .

I started on page _____ .

I ended on page _____ .

I read a total of _____ pages.

Instructions

❑ Topic/Subject:_____

❑ Read the passage and summarize what you read on the front side of this paper.

❑ Find a partner, trade papers, and read each other's summaries.

❑ Develop three test questions with your partner. You should each copy the questions on the back of your papers. Staple both papers together and turn them in.

_____

_____

_____

_____

_____

Connections

Name _____ Date _____

Daily Reading Record and Journal

_____
_____
Title

_____
Author

_____
Genre

• • • • • • • • • • • •

I started on page _____ .

I ended on page _____ .

I read a total of _____ pages.

Instructions

❏ Describe at least two connections you can make to your book.

  Text to Self   Text to Text   Text to World
  (this book to your life) (this book to another book) (this book to a world situation)

❏ Give details from the passage.

❏ Give details explaining your connections to those passages.

_____

_____

_____

_____

_____

_____

_____

Connections

Name _____ Date _____

Daily Reading Record and Journal

_____
_____
Title

_____
Author

_____
Genre

• • • • • • • • • • • •

I started on page _____ .

I ended on page _____ .

I read a total of _____ pages.

Instructions

❏ Describe at least two connections you can make to your book.

  Text to Self   Text to Text   Text to World
  (this book to your life) (this book to another book) (this book to a world situation)

❏ Give details from the passage.

❏ Give details explaining your connections to those passages.

_____

_____

_____

_____

_____

_____

_____

Connections

Name _____ Date _____

Daily Reading Record and Journal

_____

_____
Title

_____
Author

_____
Genre

• • • • • • • • • • • •

I started on page _____ .

I ended on page _____ .

I read a total of _____ pages.

Instructions

❑ Describe the best part of this story so far. Close the book and write a paragraph about it in your own words.

❑ Tell why you liked it and how it made you feel.

_____

_____

_____

_____

_____

_____

_____

_____

_____

_____

Connections

Name _____ Date _____

Daily Reading Record and Journal

_____

_____
Title

_____
Author

_____
Genre

• • • • • • • • • • • •

I started on page _____ .

I ended on page _____ .

I read a total of _____ pages.

Instructions

❑ Describe the best part of this story so far. Close the book and write a paragraph about it in your own words.

❑ Tell why you liked it and how it made you feel.

_____

_____

_____

_____

_____

_____

_____

_____

_____

_____

Connections

Name _____ Date _____

Daily Reading Record and Journal

_____

_____
Title

_____
Author

_____
Genre

• • • • • • • • • • •

I started on page _____ .

I ended on page _____ .

I read a total of _____ pages.

Instructions

(To be used with a historical, historical-fiction, or biographical book.)

❏ Write a paragraph (8–10 sentences) describing what you would have done if you had been alive and part of this historical event/story.

❏ Be sure to connect your ideas to the events of the story.

_____

_____

_____

_____

_____

_____

_____

_____

_____

- -

Connections

Score   F/NF

Name _____ Date _____

Daily Reading Record and Journal

_____

_____
Title

_____
Author

_____
Genre

• • • • • • • • • • •

I started on page _____ .

I ended on page _____ .

I read a total of _____ pages.

Instructions

(To be used with a historical, historical-fiction, or biographical book.)

❏ Write a paragraph (8–10 sentences) describing what you would have done if you had been alive and part of this historical event/story.

❏ Be sure to connect your ideas to the events of the story.

_____

_____

_____

_____

_____

_____

_____

_____

_____

Illuminating

Name _____ Date _____

Daily Reading Record and Journal

_____
Title

_____
Author

_____
Genre

• • • • • • • • • • • •

I started on page _____ .

I ended on page _____ .

I read a total of _____ pages.

Instructions

❑ Find a small passage that you want to illuminate. It can be funny, sad, exciting, a good description, an interesting part, etc.

❑ Copy a brief portion of your selection.

❑ Explain what you liked about it and why.

_____

_____

_____

_____

_____

_____

_____

_____

_____

Illuminating

Name _____ Date _____

Score   F/NF

Daily Reading Record and Journal

_____
Title

_____
Author

_____
Genre

• • • • • • • • • • • •

I started on page _____ .

I ended on page _____ .

I read a total of _____ pages.

Instructions

❑ Find a small passage that you want to illuminate. It can be funny, sad, exciting, a good description, an interesting part, etc.

❑ Copy a brief portion of your selection.

❑ Explain what you liked about it and why.

_____

_____

_____

_____

_____

_____

_____

_____

_____

Predicting

Name _____ Date _____

Score **F/NF**

_____
_____
Title

_____
Author

_____
Genre

• • • • • • • • • • •

I started on page _____.

I ended on page _____.

I read a total of _____ pages.

Daily Reading Record and Journal

Instructions

Before Reading:

❑ Re-read that last page you read and then scan the next 8–10 pages. Look for pictures, italicized or bold words, titles, clue words, etc.

❑ Predict what you think will happen in today's reading.

After Reading: (check one)

My prediction was: ____ correct ____ partially correct ____ not correct

❑ Explain what happened in today's reading and how you felt about your prediction when you were through reading.

_____
_____
_____
_____
_____

- -

Predicting

Name _____ Date _____

Score **F/NF**

_____
Title

_____
Author

_____
Genre

• • • • • • • • • • •

I started on page _____.

I ended on page _____.

I read a total of _____ pages.

Daily Reading Record and Journal

Instructions

Before Reading:

❑ Re-read that last page you read and then scan the next 8–10 pages. Look for pictures, italicized or bold words, titles, clue words, etc.

❑ Predict what you think will happen in today's reading.

After Reading: (check one)

My prediction was: ____ correct ____ partially correct ____ not correct

❑ Explain what happened in today's reading and how you felt about your prediction when you were through reading.

_____
_____
_____
_____
_____

Predicting

Name _____ Date _____

Daily Reading Record and Journal

_____

_____
Title

_____
Author

_____
Genre

. . . .

I started on page _____.

I ended on page _____.

I read a total of _____ pages.

Instructions

❑ Copy the last three to five sentences you read today.

❑ Close your book and make a prediction about what will happen next.

❑ Prove that your prediction is reasonable by presenting as much evidence (additional clues) from earlier in the story as possible.

_____
_____
_____
_____
_____
_____
_____
_____
_____

- -

Predicting

Score   F/NF

Name _____ Date _____

Daily Reading Record and Journal

_____

_____
Title

_____
Author

_____
Genre

. . . .

I started on page _____.

I ended on page _____.

I read a total of _____ pages.

Instructions

❑ Copy the last three to five sentences you read today.

❑ Close your book and make a prediction about what will happen next.

❑ Prove that your prediction is reasonable by presenting as much evidence (additional clues) from earlier in the story as possible.

_____
_____
_____
_____
_____
_____
_____
_____
_____

Questioning

Name _____ Date _____

Daily Reading Record and Journal

Instructions

While you were reading, you probably wondered about a few things:

❏ Describe what happened in the story that made you ask yourself questions.

❏ Write out the question(s) you asked yourself.

❏ Explain any answers you may have found to those questions, either in later readings or context clues that helped you infer an answer.

_____

_____

_____

_____

_____

_____

_____

_____
_____
Title

_____
Author

_____
Genre

• • • • • • • • • • • •

I started on page _____ .

I ended on page _____ .

I read a total of _____ pages.

- -

Questioning

Name _____ Date _____

Daily Reading Record and Journal

Instructions

While you were reading, you probably wondered about a few things:

❏ Describe what happened in the story that made you ask yourself questions.

❏ Write out the question(s) you asked yourself.

❏ Explain any answers you may have found to those questions, either in later readings or context clues that helped you infer an answer.

_____

_____

_____

_____

_____

_____

_____

_____
_____
Title

_____
Author

_____
Genre

• • • • • • • • • • • •

I started on page _____ .

I ended on page _____ .

I read a total of _____ pages.

Research

Name _____ Date _____

Score **NF/CA**

Daily Reading Record and Journal

_____

_____
Title

_____
Author

_____
Genre/Content Area

• • • • • • • • • • • •

I started on page _____ .

I ended on page _____ .

I read a total of _____ pages.

Instructions

❑ Topic/Person this book is about: _____

❑ Look up that person/topic in an encyclopedia and find one new fact that wasn't mentioned in your book.

❑ Explain what you learned as though you are teaching it to someone. Use supporting details.

_____

_____

_____

_____

_____

_____

- -

Research

Name _____ Date _____

Score **NF/CA**

Daily Reading Record and Journal

_____

_____
Title

_____
Author

_____
Genre/Content Area

• • • • • • • • • • • •

I started on page _____ .

I ended on page _____ .

I read a total of _____ pages.

Instructions

❑ Topic/Person this book is about: _____

❑ Look up that person/topic in an encyclopedia and find one new fact that wasn't mentioned in your book.

❑ Explain what you learned as though you are teaching it to someone. Use supporting details.

_____

_____

_____

_____

_____

_____

Research

Name ______________________________ Date ________________

Score

NF/CA

Daily Reading Record and Journal

____

____

Title

____

Author

____

Genre/Content Area

• • • • • • • • • • • • •

I started on page ________.

I ended on page ________.

I read a total of ______ pages.

Instructions

- ❑ Topic/Subject of today's reading: ______________________
- ❑ Describe the kind(s) of research an author would have to do to write about this topic and why. For example: onsite, historical records, scientific experiments, interviews, etc. You may choose and explain more than one.

____

____

____

____

____

____

____

Research

Name ______________________________ Date ________________

Score

NF/CA

Daily Reading Record and Journal

____

____

Title

____

Author

____

Genre/Content Area

• • • • • • • • • • • • •

I started on page ________.

I ended on page ________.

I read a total of ______ pages.

Instructions

- ❑ Topic/Subject of today's reading: ______________________
- ❑ Describe the kind(s) of research an author would have to do to write about this topic and why. For example: onsite, historical records, scientific experiments, interviews, etc. You may choose and explain more than one.

____

____

____

____

____

____

____

Research

Name _____ Date _____

Daily Reading Record and Journal

_____

_____
Title

_____
Author

_____
Genre/Content Area

• • • • • • • • • • • •

I started on page _____ .

I ended on page _____ .

I read a total of _____ pages.

Instructions

❏ Topic/Subject of today's reading: _____

❏ Explain how the information in this text might have been different if it had been written 10, 20, or 50 years ago. (circle one)

_____

_____

_____

_____

_____

_____

_____

_____

_____

_____

Research

Name _____ Date _____

Score   NF/CA

Daily Reading Record and Journal

_____

_____
Title

_____
Author

_____
Genre/Content Area

• • • • • • • • • • • •

I started on page _____ .

I ended on page _____ .

I read a total of _____ pages.

Instructions

❏ Topic/Subject of today's reading: _____

❏ Explain how the information in this text might have been different if it had been written 10, 20, or 50 years ago. (circle one)

_____

_____

_____

_____

_____

_____

_____

_____

_____

_____

Story Setting

Name _____ Date _____

_____

_____

Title

_____

Author

_____

Genre

• • • • • • • • • • • •

I started on page _____ .

I ended on page _____ .

I read a total of _____ pages.

Daily Reading Record and Journal

Instructions

❑ Describe the overall setting for this story.

❑ Details may include the following:

• Where (a town, another country, a farm, a kitchen) it is taking place.

• When (a year, around an important time or event) it is taking place.

• How people lived and behaved in this setting.

❑ Explain whether or not you would have enjoyed living in this setting and why.

_____

_____

_____

_____

_____

_____

- -

Story Setting

Name _____ Date _____

_____

_____

Title

_____

Author

_____

Genre

• • • • • • • • • • • •

I started on page _____ .

I ended on page _____ .

I read a total of _____ pages.

Daily Reading Record and Journal

Instructions

❑ Describe the overall setting for this story.

❑ Details may include the following:

• Where (a town, another country, a farm, a kitchen) it is taking place.

• When (a year, around an important time or event) it is taking place.

• How people lived and behaved in this setting.

❑ Explain whether or not you would have enjoyed living in this setting and why.

_____

_____

_____

_____

_____

Story Setting

Name _____ Date _____

Daily Reading Record and Journal

_____
Title

_____
Author

_____
Genre

. . . .

I started on page _____ .

I ended on page _____ .

I read a total of _____ pages.

Instructions

❑ Briefly explain the overall setting of the story. Include as many details from the story as you can remember and infer.

❑ Illustrate the setting on the back and label the details in the picture.

_____

_____

_____

_____

_____

_____

_____

_____

(Do not copy lines on the back of this page.)

- -

Story Setting

Name _____ Date _____

Daily Reading Record and Journal

_____
Title

_____
Author

_____
Genre

. . . .

I started on page _____ .

I ended on page _____ .

I read a total of _____ pages.

Instructions

❑ Briefly explain the overall setting of the story. Include as many details from the story as you can remember and infer.

❑ Illustrate the setting on the back and label the details in the picture.

_____

_____

_____

_____

_____

_____

_____

_____

(Do not copy lines on the back of this page.)

Story Setting

Name _____ Date _____

Daily Reading Record and Journal

_____

Title

_____

Author

_____

Genre

• • • • • • • • • • • •

I started on page _____ .

I ended on page _____ .

I read a total of _____ pages.

Instructions

❏ Create a graphic organizer on the back to compare and contrast the setting of the main character's life with the setting of your modern-day life. Be sure to include as many details as possible.

❏ Explain it in a brief (3–5 sentence) paragraph below.

_____

_____

_____

_____

_____

_____

_____

_____

(Do not copy lines on the back of this page.)

- -

Story Setting

Name _____ Date _____

Daily Reading Record and Journal

_____

Title

_____

Author

_____

Genre

• • • • • • • • • • •

I started on page _____ .

I ended on page _____ .

I read a total of _____ pages.

Instructions

❏ Create a graphic organizer on the back to compare and contrast the setting of the main character's life with the setting of your modern-day life. Be sure to include as many details as possible.

❏ Explain it in a brief (3–5 sentence) paragraph below.

_____

_____

_____

_____

_____

_____

_____

_____

(Do not copy lines on the back of this page.)

Story Setting

Name _____ Date _____

Daily Reading Record and Journal

_____
Title

_____
Author

_____
Genre

. . . .

I started on page _____ .

I ended on page _____ .

I read a total of _____ pages.

Instructions

❏ Describe the main setting of this story.

❏ Setting details change often in a story. Sometimes there are significant changes, and sometimes there are only minor ones. Give two to three examples from today's reading of setting changes that have occurred in your story.

_____
_____
_____
_____
_____
_____
_____
_____
_____

- -

Story Setting

Score   F/NF

Name _____ Date _____

Daily Reading Record and Journal

_____
Title

_____
Author

_____
Genre

. . . .

I started on page _____ .

I ended on page _____ .

I read a total of _____ pages.

Instructions

❏ Describe the main setting of this story.

❏ Setting details change often in a story. Sometimes there are significant changes, and sometimes there are only minor ones. Give two to three examples from today's reading of setting changes that have occurred in your story.

_____
_____
_____
_____
_____
_____
_____
_____
_____

Story Setting

Name _____ Date _____

_____

_____

Title

_____

Author

_____

Genre

. . . .

I started on page _____ .

I ended on page _____ .

I read a total of _____ pages.

Daily Reading Record and Journal

Instructions

❑ Briefly describe the setting, using details from the text.

❑ Identify any details you know about the setting that are not directly described in the text. For example, if the text mentions that it's hot outside, you can assume it's summer; or, if the setting is on a farm, you can assume there's probably a barn and some fences.

❑ Illustrate the setting on the back of this page.

_____

_____

_____

_____

_____

(Do not copy lines on the back of this page.)

- -

Story Setting

Name _____ Date _____

_____

_____

Title

_____

Author

_____

Genre

. . . .

I started on page _____ .

I ended on page _____ .

I read a total of _____ pages.

Daily Reading Record and Journal

Instructions

❑ Briefly describe the setting, using details from the text.

❑ Identify any details you know about the setting that are not directly described in the text. For example, if the text mentions that it's hot outside, you can assume it's summer; or, if the setting is on a farm, you can assume there's probably a barn and some fences.

❑ Illustrate the setting on the back of this page.

_____

_____

_____

_____

_____

(Do not copy lines on the back of this page.)

Summarizing

Name _____ Date _____

Daily Reading Record and Journal

_____

_____
Title

_____
Author

_____
Genre

• • • • • • • • • • •

I started on page _____ .

I ended on page _____ .

I read a total of _____ pages.

Instructions

❏ Outline the key events (just the most important parts) in the passage you read today.

❏ Close your book and explain in your own words what happened. (Do not copy it from your book.)

❏ Remember to use transition words. For example, *first, second, then, next, also, in the meantime, a little while later, finally,* etc.

_____

_____

_____

_____

_____

_____

_____

Summarizing

Name _____ Date _____

Daily Reading Record and Journal

_____

_____
Title

_____
Author

_____
Genre

• • • • • • • • • • •

I started on page _____ .

I ended on page _____ .

I read a total of _____ pages.

Instructions

❏ Outline the key events (just the most important parts) in the passage you read today.

❏ Close your book and explain in your own words what happened. (Do not copy it from your book.)

❏ Remember to use transition words. For example, *first, second, then, next, also, in the meantime, a little while later, finally,* etc.

_____

_____

_____

_____

_____

_____

_____

Summarizing

Score F/NF

Name _____ Date _____

Daily Reading Record and Journal

_____
_____
Title

_____
Author

_____
Genre

. . . .

I started on page _____ .

I ended on page _____ .

I read a total of _____ pages.

Instructions

Summarize your book by . . .

❑ writing 2–3 sentences to describe what happened at the beginning of the story.

❑ writing 2–3 sentences to describe what happened in the middle of the story.

❑ writing 2–3 sentences to describe what happened at the end of the story.

_____
_____
_____
_____
_____
_____

- -

Summarizing

Score F/NF

Name _____ Date _____

Daily Reading Record and Journal

_____
Title

_____
Author

_____
Genre

. . . .

I started on page _____ .

I ended on page _____ .

I read a total of _____ pages.

Instructions

Summarize your book by . . .

❑ writing 2–3 sentences to describe what happened at the beginning of the story.

❑ writing 2–3 sentences to describe what happened in the middle of the story.

❑ writing 2–3 sentences to describe what happened at the end of the story.

_____
_____
_____
_____
_____
_____

Summarizing

Score   **F/NF**

Name _____ Date _____

Daily Reading Record and Journal

_____
Title

_____
Author

_____
Genre

• • • • • • • • • • •

I started on page _____ .

I ended on page _____ .

I read a total of _____ pages.

Instructions

❑ Describe one significant event or problem/challenge the main character(s) faced.

❑ Explain how the situation was resolved.

❑ Support your answer with several pieces of evidence from the book.

_____

_____

_____

_____

_____

_____

_____

_____

_____

_____

Summarizing

Score   **F/NF**

Name _____ Date _____

Daily Reading Record and Journal

_____
Title

_____
Author

_____
Genre

• • • • • • • • • • •

I started on page _____ .

I ended on page _____ .

I read a total of _____ pages.

Instructions

❑ Describe one significant event or problem/challenge the main character(s) faced.

❑ Explain how the situation was resolved.

❑ Support your answer with several pieces of evidence from the book.

_____

_____

_____

_____

_____

_____

_____

_____

_____

Summarizing

Score | **F/NF**

Name _____ Date _____

Daily Reading Record and Journal

_____
_____
Title

_____
Author

_____
Genre

• • • • • • • • • • • •

I started on page _____ .

I ended on page _____ .

I read a total of _____ pages.

Instructions

❑ What/Who is the subject of this text: _____

❑ Use the "5Ws + H" questions (below) to help you outline the most important details of this story. Use that information to write an exciting newspaper article.

___ Who, ___ What, ___ When, ___ Where, ___ Why, + ___ How

❑ Don't forget to create an intriguing title as a headline!

_____

_____

_____

_____

_____

_____

_____

- -

Summarizing

Score | **F/NF**

Name _____ Date _____

Daily Reading Record and Journal

_____
_____
Title

_____
Author

_____
Genre

• • • • • • • • • • • •

I started on page _____ .

I ended on page _____ .

I read a total of _____ pages.

Instructions

❑ What/Who is the subject of this text: _____

❑ Use the "5Ws + H" questions (below) to help you outline the most important details of this story. Use that information to write an exciting newspaper article.

___ Who, ___ What, ___ When, ___ Where, ___ Why, + ___ How

❑ Don't forget to create an intriguing title as a headline!

_____

_____

_____

_____

_____

_____

_____

Summarizing

Score   F

Name _____ Date _____

Daily Reading Record and Journal

_____

_____
Title

_____
Author

_____
Genre

· · · · · · · · · · · ·

I started on page _____ .

I ended on page _____ .

I read a total of _____ pages.

Instructions

❑ Write a brief paragraph explaining how your story ended.

❑ Pretend that you are the author and have decided to change the ending. Rewrite it.

_____

_____

_____

_____

_____

_____

_____

_____

_____

- -

Summarizing

Score   F

Name _____ Date _____

Daily Reading Record and Journal

_____

_____
Title

_____
Author

_____
Genre

· · · · · · · · · · · ·

I started on page _____ .

I ended on page _____ .

I read a total of _____ pages.

Instructions

❑ Write a brief paragraph explaining how your story ended.

❑ Pretend that you are the author and have decided to change the ending. Rewrite it.

_____

_____

_____

_____

_____

_____

_____

_____

_____

Summarizing

Name _____ Date _____

Daily Reading Record and Journal

_____

_____
Title

_____
Author

_____
Genre

· · · · · · · · · · · ·

I started on page _____ .

I ended on page _____ .

I read a total of _____ pages.

Instructions

❑ Close your book and write a brief biography about _____ in your own words.
   (name of main character)

❑ The first paragraph should tell about his/her early years.

❑ The second paragraph should give details about important events (actions, discoveries, inventions, etc.).

❑ The third paragraph should tell about his/her later years and have a conclusion.

_____

_____

_____

_____

_____

- -

Summarizing

Name _____ Date _____

Daily Reading Record and Journal

_____

_____
Title

_____
Author

_____
Genre

· · · · · · · · · · · ·

I started on page _____ .

I ended on page _____ .

I read a total of _____ pages.

Instructions

❑ Close your book and write a brief biography about _____ in your own words.
   (name of main character)

❑ The first paragraph should tell about his/her early years.

❑ The second paragraph should give details about important events (actions, discoveries, inventions, etc.).

❑ The third paragraph should tell about his/her later years and have a conclusion.

_____

_____

_____

_____

_____

Score	F/NF

Name _____ Date _____

Daily Reading Record and Journal

_____

Title

_____

Author

_____

Genre

• • • • • • • • • • •

I started on page _____ .

I ended on page _____ .

I read a total of _____ pages.

Instructions

❑ Name the hero/heroine in your book: _____

❑ Explain in your own words what he/she did to become a hero.

❑ Support your answer with evidence from the book.

_____

_____

_____

_____

_____

_____

_____

_____

- -

Summarizing

Score	F/NF

Name _____ Date _____

Daily Reading Record and Journal

_____

Title

_____

Author

_____

Genre

• • • • • • • • • • •

I started on page _____ .

I ended on page _____ .

I read a total of _____ pages.

Instructions

❑ Name the hero/heroine in your book: _____

❑ Explain in your own words what he/she did to become a hero.

❑ Support your answer with evidence from the book.

_____

_____

_____

_____

_____

_____

_____

_____

Summarizing

Name _____ Date _____

_____

_____

Title

_____

Author

_____

Genre

• • • • • • • • • • •

I started on page _____ .

I ended on page _____ .

I read a total of _____ pages.

Daily Reading Record and Journal

Instructions

Think about the story from beginning to end, and then think about the title.

❏　Express whether you think the title does or does not fit the story.

❏　Defend your opinion using evidence from the text.

_____

_____

_____

_____

_____

_____

_____

_____

- -

Summarizing

Score　**F/NF**

Name _____ Date _____

_____

_____

Title

_____

Author

_____

Genre

• • • • • • • • • • •

I started on page _____ .

I ended on page _____ .

I read a total of _____ pages.

Daily Reading Record and Journal

Instructions

Think about the story from beginning to end, and then think about the title.

❏　Express whether you think the title does or does not fit the story.

❏　Defend your opinion using evidence from the text.

_____

_____

_____

_____

_____

_____

_____

_____

Summarizing

Name _____ Date _____

Daily Reading Record and Journal

_____
Title

_____
Author

_____
Genre/Content Area

· · · · · · · · · · · ·

I started on page _____.

I ended on page _____.

I read a total of _____ pages.

Instructions

❑ Topic/Subject of today's reading: _____

❑ Identify the three most important facts you learned today by writing three brief test questions on the front side of this page. Number each question.

❑ Number and answer each question (using complete sentences) on the back.

_____

_____

_____

_____

_____

_____

Summarizing

Name _____ Date _____

Daily Reading Record and Journal

_____
Title

_____
Author

_____
Genre/Content Area

· · · · · · · · · · · ·

I started on page _____.

I ended on page _____.

I read a total of _____ pages.

Instructions

❑ Topic/Subject of today's reading: _____

❑ Identify the three most important facts you learned today by writing three brief test questions on the front side of this page. Number each question.

❑ Number and answer each question (using complete sentences) on the back.

_____

_____

_____

_____

_____

_____

Summarizing

Score | NF/CA

Name _____ Date _____

```
_____
_____
        Title
_____
       Author
_____
   Genre/Content Area
. . . . . . . . . . . .

I started on page _____ .

I ended on page _____ .

I read a total of _____ pages.
```

Daily Reading Record and Journal

Instructions

❑ Write a sentence that identifies the "big idea" (main idea) of today's reading.

❑ Make that sentence into a paragraph by proving the "big idea" with details from the text to support it.

_____
_____
_____
_____
_____
_____
_____
_____

- -

Summarizing

Score | NF/CA

Name _____ Date _____

```
_____
_____
        Title
_____
       Author
_____
   Genre/Content Area
. . . . . . . . . . . .

I started on page _____ .

I ended on page _____ .

I read a total of _____ pages.
```

Daily Reading Record and Journal

Instructions

❑ Write a sentence that identifies the "big idea" (main idea) of today's reading.

❑ Make that sentence into a paragraph by proving the "big idea" with details from the text to support it.

_____
_____
_____
_____
_____
_____
_____
_____

Summarizing

Name _____ Date _____

Daily Reading Record and Journal

_____
Title

_____
Author

_____
Genre

• • • • • • • • • • •

I started on page _____ .

I ended on page _____ .

I read a total of _____ pages.

Instructions

❑ Who is the subject of this piece? _____

❑ Identify the interesting or important contribution(s) this person made to mankind and support your answer with examples and evidence from the passage.

❑ How have you or others benefited from his/her contribution(s)?

_____

_____

_____

_____

_____

_____

_____

- -

Summarizing

Name _____ Date _____

Daily Reading Record and Journal

_____
Title

_____
Author

_____
Genre

• • • • • • • • • • •

I started on page _____ .

I ended on page _____ .

I read a total of _____ pages.

Instructions

❑ Who is the subject of this piece? _____

❑ Identify the interesting or important contribution(s) this person made to mankind and support your answer with examples and evidence from the passage.

❑ How have you or others benefited from his/her contribution(s)?

_____

_____

_____

_____

_____

_____

_____

Summarizing

Name _____ Date _____

_____

_____
Title

_____
Author

_____
Genre/Content Area

. . . .

I started on page _____.

I ended on page _____.

I read a total of _____ pages.

Daily Reading Record and Journal

Instructions

❑ Topic/Subject of today's reading: _____

❑ Assume your friend knows nothing about the topic of your book. Write a letter to him/her sharing the information that you found to be the most interesting or most important. Make it easy to understand.

_____

_____

_____

_____

_____

_____

_____

_____

_____

Summarizing

Score   NF/CA

Name _____ Date _____

_____

_____
Title

_____
Author

_____
Genre/Content Area

. . . .

I started on page _____.

I ended on page _____.

I read a total of _____ pages.

Daily Reading Record and Journal

Instructions

❑ Topic/Subject of today's reading: _____

❑ Assume your friend knows nothing about the topic of your book. Write a letter to him/her sharing the information that you found to be the most interesting or most important. Make it easy to understand.

_____

_____

_____

_____

_____

_____

_____

_____

_____

Visualizing

Name _____ Date _____

Daily Reading Record and Journal

_____

_____
Title

_____
Author

_____
Genre

· · · · · · · · · · · ·

I started on page _____ .

I ended on page _____ .

I read a total of _____ pages.

Instructions

❑ Describe a scene from today's reading. You may copy it from the book or write it in your own words.

❑ Draw a picture on the back to illustrate what you visualized as you read.

❑ Add as many details as possible. You may also use background knowledge and information from previous passages.

_____

_____

_____

_____

_____

_____

(Do not copy lines on the back of this page.)

Visualizing

Name _____ Date _____

Score   F/NF

Daily Reading Record and Journal

_____

_____
Title

_____
Author

_____
Genre

· · · · · · · · · · · ·

I started on page _____ .

I ended on page _____ .

I read a total of _____ pages.

Instructions

❑ Describe a scene from today's reading. You may copy it from the book or write it in your own words.

❑ Draw a picture on the back to illustrate what you visualized as you read.

❑ Add as many details as possible. You may also use background knowledge and information from previous passages.

_____

_____

_____

_____

_____

_____

(Do not copy lines on the back of this page.)

Visualizing

Name _____ Date _____

Daily Reading Record and Journal

_____

_____
Title

_____
Author

_____
Genre

. . . .

I started on page _____ .

I ended on page _____ .

I read a total of _____ pages.

Instructions

❏ Name the book's illustrator: _____

❏ Study the illustrations in the book. Explain why you do or do not like them.

❏ Do the pictures match what you visualized when you were reading the story? _____ yes _____ no

_____

_____

_____

_____

_____

_____

- -

Visualizing

Name _____ Date _____

Daily Reading Record and Journal

_____

_____
Title

_____
Author

_____
Genre

. . . .

I started on page _____ .

I ended on page _____ .

I read a total of _____ pages.

Instructions

❏ Name the book's illustrator: _____

❏ Study the illustrations in the book. Explain why you do or do not like them.

❏ Do the pictures match what you visualized when you were reading the story? _____ yes _____ no

_____

_____

_____

_____

_____

_____

Word Study

Score   **F/NF**

Name _____ Date _____

Daily Reading Record and Journal

_____
Title

_____
Author

_____
Genre

· · · · · · · · · · ·

I started on page _____ .

I ended on page _____ .

I read a total of _____ pages.

Instructions

❑ Find a word you did not know. Copy the sentence in which you found it and <u>underline</u> the word.

❑ Identify any context clues in surrounding passages that might help you figure out what the word means.

❑ Tell what you think the word means and then use it in a sentence of your own.

_____

_____

_____

_____

_____

_____

- -

Word Study

Score   **F/NF**

Name _____ Date _____

Daily Reading Record and Journal

_____
Title

_____
Author

_____
Genre

· · · · · · · · · · ·

I started on page _____ .

I ended on page _____ .

I read a total of _____ pages.

Instructions

❑ Find a word you did not know. Copy the sentence in which you found it and <u>underline</u> the word.

❑ Identify any context clues in surrounding passages that might help you figure out what the word means.

❑ Tell what you think the word means and then use it in a sentence of your own.

_____

_____

_____

_____

_____

_____

Word Study

Name _____ Date _____

_____

_____

Title

_____

Author

_____

Genre

. . . .

I started on page _____ .

I ended on page _____ .

I read a total of _____ pages.

Daily Reading Record and Journal

Instructions

❑ Find a word you did not know. Copy the sentence in which you found it and <u>underline</u> the word.

❑ Use a thesaurus to find three substitute words (synonyms) for the word.

❑ Look the word up in a dictionary. Find and copy just that part of the definition that seems to fit this word.

❑ Use that word in a sentence.

_____

_____

_____

_____

_____

_____

Word Study

Name _____ Date _____

Score   F/NF

_____

_____

Title

_____

Author

_____

Genre

. . . .

I started on page _____ .

I ended on page _____ .

I read a total of _____ pages.

Daily Reading Record and Journal

Instructions

❑ Find a word you did not know. Copy the sentence in which you found it and <u>underline</u> the word.

❑ Use a thesaurus to find three substitute words (synonyms) for the word.

❑ Look the word up in a dictionary. Find and copy just that part of the definition that seems to fit this word.

❑ Use that word in a sentence.

_____

_____

_____

_____

_____

_____

Word Study

Name _____ Date _____

Daily Reading Record and Journal

_____

Title

_____

Author

_____

Genre

. . . .

I started on page _____.

I ended on page _____.

I read a total of _____ pages.

Instructions

❑ Identify an interesting word or phrase you found in your reading.

_____

❑ Use a dictionary and/or thesaurus to learn its meaning more clearly. Explain what you think it means below in your own words.

❑ Illustrate the word on the back of this page, using labels to point out details that further explain the meaning of the word.

_____

_____

_____

_____

_____

(Do not copy lines on the back of this page.)

- -

Word Study

Name _____ Date _____

Score | F/NF

Daily Reading Record and Journal

_____

Title

_____

Author

_____

Genre

. . . .

I started on page _____.

I ended on page _____.

I read a total of _____ pages.

Instructions

❑ Identify an interesting word or phrase you found in your reading.

_____

❑ Use a dictionary and/or thesaurus to learn its meaning more clearly. Explain what you think it means below in your own words.

❑ Illustrate the word on the back of this page, using labels to point out details that further explain the meaning of the word.

_____

_____

_____

_____

_____

(Do not copy lines on the back of this page.)

Word Study

Name _____ Date _____

Daily Reading Record and Journal

Instructions

❑ Topic: _____

❑ Find three or four vocabulary words in your book. They are usually listed on the first page of a chapter or found in bold print throughout the chapter. Write each word in a separate box (first column) on the chart.

❑ After you read each definition and the surrounding paragraphs, close your book and write a definition in your own words (second column).

❑ Do a quick sketch (third column) to illustrate each vocabulary word when you have finished all of reading.

Vocabulary Word	Definition	Sketch

(Copy Vocabulary Definition/Sketch chart, page 79, on the back.)

_____

_____

Title

_____

Author

_____

Content Area

• • • • • • • • • • • •

I started on page _____ .

I ended on page _____ .

I read a total of _____ pages.

Word Study

Name _____ Date _____

Score   CA

Daily Reading Record and Journal

Instructions

❑ Topic: _____

❑ Find three or four vocabulary words in your book. They are usually listed on the first page of a chapter or found in bold print throughout the chapter. Write each word in a separate box (first column) on the chart.

❑ After you read each definition and the surrounding paragraphs, close your book and write a definition in your own words (second column).

❑ Do a quick sketch (third column) to illustrate each vocabulary word when you have finished all of reading.

Vocabulary Word	Definition	Sketch

(Copy Vocabulary Definition/Sketch chart, page 79, on the back.)

_____

Title

_____

Author

_____

Content Area

• • • • • • • • • • • •

I started on page _____ .

I ended on page _____ .

I read a total of _____ pages.

Word Study

Name _____ Date _____

Daily Reading Record and Journal

Instructions

❏ Topic/Subject: _____

❏ Find three to four vocabulary words. They are usually listed on the first page of a chapter or found in bold print throughout the chapter.

❏ After you read each definition and the surrounding paragraphs, close your book and use each word in a sentence. Be sure to <u>underline</u> the vocabulary word in each sentence.

_____

Title

_____

Author

_____

Content Area

• • • • • • • • • • •

I started on page _____ .

I ended on page _____ .

I read a total of _____ pages.

_____

_____

_____

_____

_____

_____

_____

- -

Word Study

Name _____ Date _____

Daily Reading Record and Journal

Instructions

❏ Topic/Subject: _____

❏ Find three to four vocabulary words. They are usually listed on the first page of a chapter or found in bold print throughout the chapter.

❏ After you read each definition and the surrounding paragraphs, close your book and use each word in a sentence. Be sure to <u>underline</u> the vocabulary word in each sentence.

_____

Title

_____

Author

_____

Content Area

• • • • • • • • • • •

I started on page _____ .

I ended on page _____ .

I read a total of _____ pages.

_____

_____

_____

_____

_____

_____

_____

Free Response

Name _____ Date _____

Daily Reading Record and Journal

_____

_____
Title

_____
Author

_____
Genre/Content Area

· · · · · · · · · · · · ·

I started on page _____ .

I ended on page _____ .

I read a total of _____ pages.

Instructions

Today, you may choose what you would like to write about in response to your reading. Your score will be dependent on a thoughtful, detailed response that is supported by evidence from your text.

_____

_____

_____

_____

_____

_____

_____

- -

Free Response

Score _____

Name _____ Date _____

Daily Reading Record and Journal

_____

_____
Title

_____
Author

_____
Genre/Content Area

· · · · · · · · · · · · ·

I started on page _____ .

I ended on page _____ .

I read a total of _____ pages.

Instructions

Today, you may choose what you would like to write about in response to your reading. Your score will be dependent on a thoughtful, detailed response that is supported by evidence from your text.

_____

_____

_____

_____

_____

_____

_____

_____

Open Form

Name _____ Date _____

_____

_____

Title

_____

Author

_____

Genre/Content Area

• • • • • • • • • • • •

I started on page _____ .

I ended on page _____ .

I read a total of _____ pages.

Daily Reading Record and Journal

Instructions

❑ _____

_____

❑ _____

_____

❑ _____

_____

❑ _____

_____

Respond using the back of this page.

- -

Open Form

Name _____ Date _____

Score _____

_____

_____

Title

_____

Author

_____

Genre/Content Area

• • • • • • • • • • • •

I started on page _____ .

I ended on page _____ .

I read a total of _____ pages.

Daily Reading Record and Journal

Instructions

❑ _____

_____

❑ _____

_____

❑ _____

_____

❑ _____

_____

Respond using the back of this page.

Daily Reading Record and Journal

Week of _____

Name _____

- -

Daily Reading Record and Journal

Book _____

Name _____

Additional Lines

_____

_____

_____

_____

_____

_____

_____

_____

_____

- -

Additional Lines

_____

_____

_____

_____

_____

_____

_____

_____

_____

_____

T-Graph

Title:	Title:
•	•
•	•

- -

T-Graph

Title:	Title:
•	•
•	•

Vocabulary/Definition/Sketch Chart

Vocabulary Word	Definition	Sketch

Vocabulary/Definition/Sketch Chart

Vocabulary Word	Definition	Sketch

KWL Chart

What I **K**now	What I **W**ant to Know	What I **L**earned

- -

KWL Chart

What I **K**now	What I **W**ant to Know	What I **L**earned